The
PATHWAY *to*
HEALING
is PAINFUL

A Story for
God's Glory

Cheryl Hollinshead

TRILOGY
A WHOLLY OWNED SUBSIDIARY OF TBN
PROFESSIONAL PUBLISHING MEETS POWERFUL PROMOTION

Trilogy Christian Publishers
A Wholly Owned Subsidiary of Trinity Broadcasting Network
2442 Michelle Drive
Tustin, CA 92780

10 9 8 7 6 5 4 3 2 1
Library of Congress Cataloging-in-Publication Data is available.
ISBN 979-9-89041-919-4
ISBN (ebook) 979-9-89041-920-0

Dedication

This book is dedicated to my beloved Savior, Jesus Christ, my Father Abba, and the Holy Spirit, for guidance and never leaving nor forsaking me—even when I did not have understanding nor deserve this unmerited favor of God, the Great I AM.

For all the trials and triumphs that brought me to where I am today, every beautiful piece of the tapestry woven together to create all this story, for His Glory—it has been a tumultuous road, but one that is well worth every scar, every bruise, every scrape, and every wound. I praise Him for all He has done for me. May some small piece of my life be a reflection of my gratitude to Him.

Foreword

Life is more difficult than I would prefer. The joy of life is not found in the absence of conflict or elimination of problems. Cheryl Hollinshead has written an honest, heart-felt account of her journey. The reader is invited to a pathway of discovery. Some of the difficulty and pain may be familiar. My prayer is that the triumph of faith and purpose described in these pages will become the story of all who read this remarkable book. I have known Cheryl for many years. I have often been amazed at her indomitable spirit. I am grateful she has invested the effort to share a bit of her story. God is no respecter of persons; He is still restoring lives in the midst of a broken world.

—Pastor Allen Jackson,
World Outreach Church, Murfreesboro, Tennessee

As a professional counselor for over 30 years and the Clinical Director of Branches, I have walked with hundreds of people through their pain and stories. Specializing in trauma, I have heard hours and hours of heartbreaking stories. Cheryl's story is one that has touched me in a powerful way. I have had the privilege of working for years with Cheryl in her journey of healing. Cheryl endured abuse and neglect which led to unhealthy coping skills in her younger years. She took these experiences and the prompting from the Holy Spirit to turn her life around. Her honest account of her life and how to pursue health is more than inspiring. She has always wanted to glorify God and show His light. This book is another way she is sharing God's love. Reading this book will encourage you in your physical, intellectual, emotional, and spiritual health. Even in her end of life journey, she continues to be a reflection of Jesus. I pray blessings over you as you read this wonderful account of a loving, healthy life.

—Tracey Robison,
LPC-MHSP

Acknowledgements

I would like to take the time to acknowledge several people:

- My brother, who I have grieved for silently for many years. He died at the young age of thirty-nine (when I was spared), leaving behind four children, masking the deep pains I knew he had and could not escape.

- My nephew, who followed in his father's footsteps at the early age of thirty-five. I did not have a relationship close enough to either of them to have made a difference.

- Every person who ever prayed for me.

- All those who spoke against me, I thank God for you.

- My daughter, my Baby Girl, who has been through it all with me, from my pregnancy at sixteen years old. I love you, Baby Girl! I would fight a lion, a bear, and Satan himself for you—and do so daily, on my knees and often walking (and sometimes shouting) in the spiritual realm. Thank you for accepting me with all my flaws, for allowing me to make amends for all my mess-ups, and for allowing me to still be a mom to you, even at this late stage in life.

- My grandfather, for giving me the gift of a safe place as a small child in the redwoods of California on my fifth birthday.

- My dearest Kathy and Roger (who I call Mom and Dad), because they came into my life at a time when I was floundering and couldn't catch a breath. They loved me unconditionally, and I slowly learned to do the same. I did not have to perform, for once in my life. Oh, the burden of carrying that around. For my fiftieth birthday, they took me back to the redwoods for horseback riding, the beach, whale watching, and to ride the biggest roller coaster. It was EPIC, and it was the best birthday ever since that time when I was five.

- Brenda T., I miss you. I know Kathy and Roger because of you. You had the kindest heart, and we had so much laughter, and the best prayer walks in the stairwells.

- L2, I miss you. You gave me 2 Timothy, chapter 1, verse 7 in 2001, and I have never forgotten it. For every three seconds I spoke it out loud, it was three seconds the enemy did not have control. I still know it and say it: *For God did not give me a spirit of fear, but of power, love, and a sound mind!* You told me that everything was for a reason, a season, or for life.

- My sister, who wanted to protect me when she couldn't, and told me, "It's not your fault you're sick."

- Sheila, who gave me the nickname "Bag Lady" long before we knew how appropriately it would fit.

- All the people who have poured into me, prayed for me, and supported me, I thank you.

- Julie and Jim, for being my encouragers, walking, praying, being spiritual mentors and friends.

- My extraordinary Bible study group and friends.

- My recovery group and 12-step leader, Kristin.

- Ruth, for her wisdom, prayer, and chips!

- My "Girl Gang."

- My never-the-less morning prayer family.

- My Friday night prayer group.

- My nieces and nephews, who I have a heart for more than they know.

- My CWIMA group and my CBS Bible study.

- My amazing counselor, Tracey, who has the sweetest spirit and demeanor of anyone I think I have ever met. I love her patience, wisdom, godly instruction, and truthfulness.

- Christina Cartoon, and my amazing hairdresser extraordinaire, Heather!

- My pastor and his wife, as well as his parents, for their steadfast faith in serving the Lord. It really does matter and make a difference—just ask my husband, who used to set up chairs in the old hotel, long before they got the property with a tent.

- Grandma Brenda, for being good to Papa Jim and all the grands.

- My new writing group, who has welcomed me so graciously.

- Susan Seiling, who helped make this project a reality. Without Susan's encouragement, energy, and belief, this would not have been possible. And I thank Juliana for introducing us. God really is in all the details.

- Ryan Bowen, who filmed my testimony video for Branches.

- My mother and father, for giving me life and teaching me perseverance, survival, work ethic, how to take care of what I have been given, and how to make a penny stretch into a dollar.

- If I have left anyone out, please know that it is not intentional.

What I may have lacked in resources, I learned to make up in work ethic and resourcefulness. Once I surrendered my life to the Lord, it all became an offering. Nothing is ever wasted with the Father of all. I have been saved by grace, and have been allowed to live, by His mercy, that I might be made pure and holy, spotless and blameless before Him.

He is coming for a bride who is pure and clean. I am. My life is an offering. I am a spotted goat. I may have been living and saying, "I know who Jesus is," but have I truly submitted myself in relationship to Him? Am I continually walking under His shed blood so I may be presented as a spotless, blameless lamb—as an offering? There is a difference. It requires relinquishing your will, a relationship, humility, and submission—but it comes with ever greater eternal rewards!

We have to be covered under the blood of Jesus to be presented as holy—and it may have been a free invitation to us, but it cost Him EVERYTHING!!! May I never forget the cost that pulled me from the muck and mire, or allow the small stuff of time to block my view of eternity.

Table of Contents

Dedication 5

Foreword 7

Acknowledgements 9

Prologue 17

Chapter One: *Always Been a Fighter!* 23

Chapter Two: *The Spiritual Side of Things* 29

Chapter Three: *My New Friends* 35

Chapter Four: *Alone Again* 39

Chapter Five: *By Works* 43

Chapter Six: *My Plans* 49

Chapter Seven: *Choices* 59

Chapter Eight: *I Am Still Broken* 71

Chapter Nine: *Don't Let the Makeup
and Jewelry Fool You* 79

Chapter Ten: *Healing: A Short Trip and
a Long Journey* 89

Chapter Eleven: *Healing Roads* 95

Chapter Twelve: *Embodied Prayer
and Healing Movement* 105

Conclusion 115

Helpful Prayers and Affirmations 119

Helpful Videos 125

Prologue

And we know that in all things God works for the good of those who love him, who have been called according to his purpose. (Romans 8:28)

Some of my greatest memories come from when I was very young.

I think of a time when I had peace, joy, and contentment. Ahhhh, you know the kind—as though there is nothing that can come near you. The kind where you lie back on a blanket under a shade tree on a fall day, and the tree is bursting with colors of red and orange, and the smell – it's crisp. The air – you can feel it; the breeze even feels different. The sun is warm on your skin, but never hot.

Sipping apple cider, roasting marshmallows on firepits, hiking in the woods.

Trick or treating with all my neighborhood friends and carving pumpkins. Then, drying the seeds and eating them. Filling pillowcases with candy, and then Dad trying all the best candy to "make sure it doesn't have razor blades or poison." (Like he wouldn't die if he ate those, too?!) We had some of the best homemade costumes you ever saw, and some of the shadiest, too. My favorite was Casper the Friendly Ghost because he was friendly. Later in this book, that will make sense. Remember, this prologue is about happy thoughts.

What about the pool in summer, and endless bike riding?

Oh, my word, how I LOVED the 70s music, and I still do. "Take it to the limit, one more time," by the Eagles.

Watermelon seed fights, filling your mouth as full as you could and then spitting them at each other like a torpedo.

Capturing fireflies in jars at night. Not having to come home until the streetlights came on.

Playing in the hot summer rain in the puddles, and riding our Big Wheels into the water down the hill, as fast as we could.

We used to have marching bands in the streets, with pots, and pans, and bushel baskets. A girl down the street had a baton and would be the leader.

We were so creative with what we had available. We made a skateboard from the metal skates you strapped to your feet and a two-by-four piece of wood. Trust me—it was not safe.

How I loved winter! We lived in a small town outside of Dayton, Ohio. I loved snow and Christmas. It was absolutely magical—except I wanted colored flashing lights on the tree, and our mom always said, "No! White lights only!" I also remember a little manger set. I would play with the baby Jesus. We went Christmas caroling in our neighborhood – just kids. It was probably the same group in the made-up marching band. My favorite carol was "Silent Night."

We went ice skating with my best friend and her family. I knew how to ice skate before I could roller skate.

When I was a small child, from the ages of about four to eight, we visited my grandparents every summer. We would spend a week at each set's home. One grandmother was a riot. She made me snap beans with her, and then she would sit and play Monopoly with us. I got to drink coffee with my grandpa, and we listened to Harry Belafonte records as they sat, and talked, and smoked 120 cigarettes. My other grandmother never learned to drive a car. She baked cookies and called us "kiddies."

You can only imagine where my life might go from these magical moments. After all—like it or not, accept it or not, realize it or not—we are all a product of whatever "normal" we grow up in. Our "normal" is what we know. In the midst of all of these joyful memories was a messed up, fallen world I had no clue about. The more I tried to understand it, the more confused I became.

So, let's go on a journey, a pathway. But be aware and know that this healing journey is paved with some pain. But know this, too: When we are done, we will make it. We won't quit. We won't stop. We won't give up. We won't give in! We will fix *"our eyes on Jesus, the Author and Perfector of our faith, who for the joy set before him endured the cross, despising the shame, and has sat down at the right hand of the throne of God."* (Hebrews 12:2)

My grandpa, my mother's dad (who was also known as "J bird"), built an iron swing set. I can remember playing on it for hours. However, all my memories on that swing were not so great.

You see, in our home it was thought to be funny to tease, make fun of, and torture the younger children, or anyone with a disadvantage. I happened to be the younger one. As I grew up, I believed I was the one who was disadvantaged – the key word is "believed." In Proverbs, it says that we are as we think we are (Proverbs 23:7), and we eat the fruit of our words (Proverbs 18:20-21).

Another phrase I was told often is, "Pretty is as pretty does." (This one is not in the Bible). Hearing that phrase began a very long life of performance for me, starting at a very young age.

We lived in a low-income neighborhood in Union, Ohio. The houses were built on some kind of a grant system. There was no air conditioning, and the basements were unfinished. But I didn't know any differently—I thought it was great!

We ate goulash, beans and cornbread, mashed potatoes and meatloaf, and then fried mashed potato cakes. Then there was the gross tuna casserole. It had crumbled potato chips on top of tuna, noodles, and peas, all mixed in with cream of mushroom soup. Eeew!

Dinner time in our home was the most dreaded time of day, mostly because if we reached across the table, our knuckles were cracked with a knife.

My brother gagged on peas and was forced to sit in the dark and eat them cold (except for when I snuck in and fed them to the dog or ate them myself).

Years later, we found out someone older let the dog lick all the plates clean and then they put them in the cabinets without actually washing them. Guess what? We survived!

Every meal was about saying, "Please pass the (food)."

"May I please be excused from the table?"

"Don't do that!"

"There are children in Africa starving to death. Clean your plate!" No offense, but at the age of four to seven, I did not know where Africa was. Also, if I had not eaten the food, would my parents have drop shipped it to them? I have since learned that, whether we eat it and don't need it, or throw food away, it is wasteful.

A little more about food and me: When I started kindergarten, I began getting very sick with vomiting and constipation. I had ulcers at age five. I remember going to dinner with my family, and we met my grandmother, aunt, and uncle at an Italian restaurant, and I got sick. I did not eat spaghetti sauce for probably fifteen years after that—only noodles with butter and salt.

The doctor told my mother it was my fault. I was making myself sick. She should leave me at school whenever I got sick. Eventually, the ulcer healed. However, I could not use a public restroom for probably twenty years. I never understood why or what I did to make myself so sick. As I got much older, I would eventually figure all of this out. My kookie sense of humor must have come from the constant reminder that it is better to laugh than to cry—as you may have already recognized.

CHAPTER ONE

Always Been a Fighter!

As long as I can remember, I was a scrappy thing—a fighter, a survivor. Something deep inside me said, "Just watch me! I can do it! Don't tell me I can't! Don't push me in a corner! Don't challenge me! Don't try me! Don't hurt me!"

If I saw someone hurting someone else, that is when SHE came out. Now, I am not sure who SHE was (or "HER," as my daughter called it), but now HER is gone, for the most part.

Let me share some of the stories about HER and SHE, and where they would show up.

I always liked to go where I was not supposed to go and do what I was not supposed to do. Now, I am sure no one reading this is like that, right? I believe the Word of God calls this "rebellion," but I did not know the truth of that word until many years later.

I have been told that, when I was a baby, there was a

young girl who would come into my nursery and pinch me until I would scream. Then, she would run. I also would take my diapers and smear the poo in them all over the front porch. The mailman slipped in it. Oops! As Forrest Gump says, "It happens." After my father cleaned it up, I never did it again (at least that's the story I was told).

I would play on the rock piles with the boys and come home with a black eye. Why? Because I was told, "Don't go out there and play," but I did it anyway. I played in the brick pile on the patio when I was not supposed to, and had to go to the doctor for emergency stitches. Why? Because I did what I was not supposed to do.

Once, I wanted a certain pair of denim tennis shoes so badly. My best friend had a pair. They had thick rubber soles with a navy stripe, and they were COOL! I am sure my mother had to do some sort of finagling to get them (we were not financially well to do, though I never knew that at the time). Once I had the shoes, I went where I was not supposed to go, and a kid (we'll call him B.W.) took my shoes and threw them away. One landed on top of a house, and I have no idea where the other went. I had a BAD habit of not wearing my shoes. I got grounded to my room for three days in my pajamas that summer for that offense. I had to eat in my room, and only got to come out for bathroom breaks. I was five years old. My best friend would walk by my house and wave to me from the sidewalk. I don't know what was worse: Not having my shoes, my friend being interrogated about the incident, or being in prison in my room.

I grew to really dislike B.W. a lot. (I have since forgiven him, and I pray for Him as someone surely prayed for me. I assure you, as you will see through the pages of the story to come, it is only by grace that we are saved, so that no man may boast (Ephesians 2:8).)

I ended up in the second grade with B.W., and my teacher made us sit next to each other. (How could she? Did she know what he did to me?) He and I conspired against her. We got our gray, wide-lined spelling paper, and wrote our spelling words as far apart as we could. We fit four words to a page. HA! We showed her not to sit us next to each other! Then it happened. My lifelong struggle with red ink began. She handed our spelling papers back. Our spelling and handwriting were perfect, but she wrote "PAPER WASTERS" in great big letters next to a GIANT frowny face.

We both laughed hard when we got those back, and it has been a source of laughter for years. But the truth was it put a scar in my mind that told me I was a BAD, red ink, frowny face, paper waster! I finally got freedom from red ink when I was forty-eight years old. I had to pray and get free from this disapproval. I may have joked around about it, but the truth is that I felt pain every time I saw it on something I did—as if a part of me was still broken. The Bible says, *"Therefore, there is now no condemnation for those who are in Christ Jesus"* (Romans 8:1).

Isn't it amazing what we buy into? The small lie, the one word, the single sentence that traps us? Jesus said the truth will set you free (John 8:32). I believe that. It's powerful to take every thought captive into the obedience of Christ (2 Corinthians 10:5).

I made so many mistakes based on the lies I believed for so long. I won't say I wish I knew then what I know now—because if I did, I would not have the tapestry for the story that weaves my life for His glory.

Let's move on to some of my real fighting. Now, remember my brother and sister showed no mercy on me, their younger sibling. I am sure it was much like almost any other home. My brother suffered from some challenges as a kid—hyperactive disorder, scoliosis, lazy eye, asthma, and I don't know what else. Kids made fun of him, and I did not like it. If he had a hyperactive attack (as I would call it), he would legitimately try to kill my sister and me with hedge trimmers, Coke bottles (we didn't have cans back then), or whatever else he could find. On more than one occasion, he punched me in the stomach and knocked the wind out of me. Living with a brother like that really helped my survival skills, I am sure.

We had neighbor kids named the G boys. They were beating up my brother one day. I decided I would take up for him and got me an equalizer – a croquet mallet. I thought, "Ha! I will teach you to pick on my brother!" Then I knocked them in the head.

There was also the big bully of the neighborhood, Big B. He would call my brother "retard," and make fun of him because he rode the short bus. There were sewer system lids on the corners, and one day I happened to be out walking alone. Big B was sitting on the curb with his fingers in the crack of that giant lid. Yes, you probably guessed it—I jumped on it, crushed all his fingers, then ran like lightning. I was so proud. Can you believe it? I was proud!

Unfortunately, my fighting continued past early grade school, all the way up into adulthood. I had a hair-pulling fight coaxed by a neighbor kid when I was in third grade. Then I had a fight with a girl who was about three years older than me when I was in fourth grade. In seventh grade, I got in my first real fist fight with a girl in twelfth grade named C.D. Half the neighborhood showed up. Once again, C.D. was a bully to people, and I decided I would just rare up.

I did these acts at home, too, with my stepfather and my mother. It happened at school with teachers. I did not care who it was; if someone wanted a fight, I gave it to them. I think I gave it to them even if they didn't want it.

I believe now that the source of that fighting was from my inability to protect myself as a child from abuse, and it made its way out any way it could. I just wasn't aware yet.

CHAPTER TWO

The Spiritual Side of Things

There were games we played as kids. At least, I thought they were games. We also went to peoples' houses, and groups of us would say stuff and levitate each other "as light as a feather." We played board games where you asked questions and waited for answers. This started from the time I was five or six to at least sixteen, and it was nothing to joke about or mess around with. Whether we realized it or not, we were engaging with dangerous, evil spirits.

In Ephesians 6:12-13, the Word tells us that we war not against flesh and blood, but against principalities, AGAINST POWERS, against rulers of the darkness of this world, and against spiritual wickedness in high places. It goes on to tell us we need to put on the whole armor of God so we can withstand the evil day, doing all we can to stand.

Since I was not brought up in a Christian home, I was

unaware of the abilities of these evil forces. But I was familiar with them, for sure. I recognized those spiritual forces as I became older and saw more. Now I am fully aware of the spiritual realm. I walk in the Spirit of the Lord, and pray, and seek His guidance. Remember when I spoke earlier about Casper the Friendly Ghost? I really think God planted that seed in my heart, helping me recognize good spirits versus evil spirits, long before I knew they actually existed.

When I was little, I wrote on the wall with—you guessed it—RED ink. My mother came and asked me why I did that. I vividly remember telling her my Uncle Carl's spirit made me do it. But he was not dead. I later found out he was into Scientology, did not believe in Jesus, and was a very bitter person. There was definitely some spiritual warfare taking place.

When I was eight, my father was transferred from Ohio to Huntsville, Alabama. That was a huge culture shock. We lived there for six to nine months, then he was transferred to Tennessee. While in Alabama, we went through two or three tornadoes. I saw a ghost enter my brother's room. I was literally run over by a bike on my way to school. My brother tore a door off its hinges with his bike. My mother got a rusty nail stuck in her foot. My mother locked herself and my sister in the bathroom and beat her with a wet washrag. We couldn't get in to rescue her. My father built a tree house, and it was filled with slugs. Those are the fond memories of that place, and then we had to move.

We stayed in a hotel for four weeks, looking for a house. When we finally found a house in Tennessee, it was not a good situation. We were only in the house a year, and my parents fought nonstop. My dad made us cut firewood with him. I was eight or nine, and we had to go all day and stack wood. We literally had thirty-five ricks of wood in our two-acre yard. We had to sleep together on the floor of the den, in front of the fire, hanging blankets over the doors of the rest of the house, to save heat and money. It was a five-bedroom house, and he didn't want to spend money to heat it. I'm not sure why he bought it.

My parents tried to take us to church during the short time we lived in the houses in Tennessee and Alabama. Mostly what I remember is them fighting all morning, then cramming into my dad's truck because he was going to "make us be a family."

It was kind of like dinner time, when we'd all be together and he'd say, "Clean your plate! Eat your food!" One time my mom was not home for dinner, and my sister had to make dinner. She was only thirteen, and didn't know what to cook. My father was so mad. We laugh about it now—especially since my husband has never had Spam.

The biggest fight my mom and dad ever had (that I saw) was after cutting wood. Mom did not have food for Dad when we got home, and they started yelling and throwing dishes in the kitchen. My brother went outside. I said, "Aren't you going to do anything?" He sat on a rock and said, "No." I marched my sassy, red-ink writing butt in there, jumped right in and screamed "What the H-E-double-hockey-sticks is wrong with you?" My mother went to the couch, lay down, and cried. I don't remember where my father went, but the fighting stopped.

My mom started driving a school bus. She found some friends and met some people, and that was pretty much where it all went downhill. Some guy came and plowed snow off our driveway, and we all disliked him greatly. Within six months, my mom was seeing him. We moved eight times in the first two years after my parents divorced, and it was the beginning of what I call, "From Ozzy and Harriet to Ozzy Osbourne."

You can't open doors and let things in (like I did when I played those "games" with my friends) and expect that there won't be any repercussions.

As a side note, we did use very many four-letter words in our home. It was a part of our normal language. Remember, whatever you grow up with is your "normal." It took me about forty-seven years to figure that out. Then it took a few more years to realize you have to allow people to come to their own realizations, through the Holy Spirit, with prayer and Jesus. I finally figured out, as Joyce Meyer used to say "I am not Holy Ghost Junior." The Word says manipulation is not a good thing, and that rebellion is as the sin of witchcraft (Deuteronomy 18:10-12).

Deuteronomy, chapter 30, verse 19 says, *"This day I call the heavens and the earth as witnesses against you that I have set before you life and death, blessing and curses. Now choose life, so that you and your children may live."* I want to choose to speak life and live with the best attitude that I can.

When we rebel against God, we are like the Israelites in the desert. But we all have our own desert season, whether it be forty years or forty days. My assignment is to pray, encourage, and point to the One who can, not try to BE the One—because I never will be, nor will I ever have all the answers. But Jesus and the infallible Word of God do.

Only Jesus can fill the void that is so deep within each of us. I did not know how deep the void was, nor did I know I was trying to fill it. But I did try to fill it—with anything and everything I could find.

CHAPTER THREE

My New Friends

I was about eleven and in sixth grade. My mother had a man living with us who was a raging alcoholic. He moved in and out like the door opens and closes. We moved almost as much. She couldn't keep a job. He took our child support, which she hid in the freezer. She worked between nursing home and correctional officer jobs. I had been coming home alone since I was nine. Then one day she came in and said, "I've given fifteen years to this family, and it's my turn. I am done." And with that, she was.

When my parents split, my father moved out in the dark so the neighbors would not see. As he drove away, his couch flew off in the middle of the road—humiliation for him.

I remember him having NOTHING but a twin bed, a black-and-white TV, and a round table. At one point, he lived in a hotel that had rats. That was because he paid my mother $800 a month in the late 1970s. The situation was ugly. I so often heard people say, "It was such an ugly divorce." As I write this, I have the cocked head look of a dog on my face as I think, "Is there a good divorce?"

Mark, chapter 10, verse 9 says, *"Therefore what God has joined together, let no one separate."* There are tremors that come from divorce that last generations, and I believe children end up in the crossfire as collateral damage. I don't think God hates us, but I do believe He hates divorce and the sin in us, and what it has produced.

Around this time, I met some new friends: Winston, Miller, Bud, and Jack were a few of them. Then I met Black Beauty, Ms. Q., Ms. Mary Jane, and then Mr. R. These became my full-time companions. I smoked, drank, and took pills from the time I was eleven until I was sixteen and became pregnant.

I was alone almost all the time. I had a couple of friends I hung with in the sixth grade, and we were heavily into a board game of the talking type: Ouija (If you are not aware, "Ouija" is the name of a demon spirit. This is also a good time to point out that we must renounce any affiliation with past curses in our life—whether ours or generational, including playing with "games" like a Ouija board. Break the chains and don't open doors. If we give the enemy a toe hold, he can get a foot hold, and that leads to a choke hold, which leads to a strong hold.) At that time, I had a Bible, but I believed as my friends did, and unfortunately that was not in God, but that we were "evolved."

I tried to run away. I packed a suitcase, walked about five miles in the dark, and met my friends at a gas station. We used a pay phone to call a cab to take us to Nashville, where we would catch a bus to go to St. Louis. The man who owned the store threatened to call the police if we didn't call our parents. At the time, I was mad. But now I can see how God intervened. Who knows what might have happened if we had gotten in a cab and gone to Nashville at eleven years old? Would we have even made it to the bus station or St. Louis?

I called my mother and told her if her boyfriend did not move out, I would. Well, I did. I called my dad, packed a bag, and went to his one-bedroom apartment. That didn't last long. He took me back to her.

She then took me to Ohio, where she left me with my grandmother for a few weeks, and she left my sister and brother home alone for weeks. We didn't know where she went. When I went to my grandmother's, I had two weeks of school left. My mother pulled me out, took me to Ohio, and made me go to school six more weeks with people I didn't know. I hated my life.

I ate a lot during this time to stuff my feelings down. Somehow, I got ahold of her diet pills that summer and figured out what bulimia and anorexia were. Boy, did my brain rush on it. I found out many years later, when I admitted myself to a hospital at twenty-three, that the same chemical reaction occurs during binging and purging as when you drink alcohol. There are so many things we do, not knowing the consequences. Deception will always come to you dressed up in a pretty package with a bit of truth—just enough to get you to take the first bite. Just like Eve in the garden, when the serpent said, "Surely God didn't say you could not eat from any tree in the garden…"

That summer after sixth grade, I lost thirty pounds, got a boyfriend, and was getting settled. Then BAM! My mother got back with her boyfriend and moved us back to Tennessee. Needless to say, I kept some of my friends: Jack and Winston. I also had some new ones: Marlboro, Michelob, and a few others.

My sister left home at sixteen in the process. Who could blame her? She was not about to go back to that house with him there. I was not aware at the time what had been done to her. She left to elope with her boyfriend and live with his parents while she finished high school. I continued to spend years with my new friends. I was alone so much, left to survive, fight, and defend myself. But looking back now, I have to say I see how the Lord used what the enemy meant for harm and used it for good. It gave me what I needed to live.

CHAPTER FOUR

Alone Again

When we moved back to Tennessee, we looked like the Beverly Hillbillies. Our stuff was piled up high on the back of a truck, and it looked like it would fall off. I was crying my eyes out because I didn't want to go back. I was settled in Ohio. I was happy there, finally away from my mother's boyfriend and his alcoholism. I had friends. I was skinny and tan. I finally felt like I belonged somewhere, then she moved us.

My brother and I got dumped at my dad's until she found a place. She lived in a pull-behind trailer on a farm, and then in a motel. Then we moved in with her and lived in a couple more houses. We were often left alone and no one knew where we were. My grandmother and aunt flew in from California and Ohio to try to help the best they knew how. They had a meeting with my dad because my brother and I were staying with random people so we could eat. Our stepdad was always drinking up the money. My mother told my father to come get us, or she would send us to a home. My father had my mother sign us over—like a transaction. We sat at the table with them while they signed the papers. Not only were we aware of the brokenness, but we had to see it in writing—a contract. I believe that children become the collateral damage of divorce.

Sometimes I didn't see my mother for months. I realize now, more than ever, that hurting people hurt people.

When I moved in with my dad, it wasn't much different, in terms of being alone. I got up at 7 a.m., then woke him up for work. I got ready for school and left. I came home to an empty house. At thirteen, I had a job babysitting after school, on weekends, and at a Dairy Queen. I did my laundry and my dad's laundry, cleaned the house, and cut the grass. Most days, my dad did not come home until 11 p.m. He worked retail, went out with friends, and modeled.

My brother played sports until he couldn't anymore because of an injury. Then he hung out with his friends and played in a band all the time. He was never home, so it was just me. I never realized how much time I spent alone until I really sat and journaled, working through a lot of life's challenges and choices. I was alone even when I was small, since my sister and brother were close to each other, and I was not close to them. Those types of bonds weren't fostered in our home. I think that is where the core feeling of rejection stemmed from, along with many other situations when I was left alone or forgotten.

So often, the voice in my head says, "You are not good enough," "Nobody really loves you," "You always mess things up," "When are you going to get it right?" or "You can't even get that right!" But God's Word says we are sons and daughters of the Most High God.

Jesus had to come and sacrifice for us because we are so incapable—ALL of us. Not just me, or you, but ALL of us. We all fall short of the glory of God. Ephesians, chapter 2, verses 8 to 10 tell us, *"For it is by grace you have been saved, through faith—and this not from yourselves; it is the gift of God—not by works, so that no one can boast. For we are God's handiwork, created in Christ Jesus to do good works, which God prepared in advance for us to do."*

I will talk more about my works next—it will take a whole chapter to cover that!

CHAPTER FIVE

By Works

I was always a worker (performance, performance, performance!). When I was very young, before I was in kindergarten, I would go with my mother to clean houses. I can remember helping her and running to have her check to see how well I made the beds. Who does that?

I would stack all the silverware in the kitchen drawer, then go get my mother so she could look at it. On my way, my brother and sister would knock it over and laugh.

I almost always kept a clean room and made my bed. My clothes had to be neat. The exception was the few years of my extreme rebellion, around age thirteen or fourteen, when I smoked in my room, had my dirty clothes piled on the floor, and didn't make my bed before school. I just shut my door, locked myself in, and made sure everything else was in order. Outside of that brief period of time, I would fold all my clothes in the drawers by color code. I also color coded the clothes I hung in my closet. Every home I've ever had, people have asked, "Is it staged?" or "Who staged it?" I always look at them, confused, and think, "Doesn't everyone live like this?"

I cleaned so much, I took the finish off my bathroom fixtures and the paint off my toilets. I vacuumed two times a day—I wanted the marks in my carpet when I woke up in the morning and when I came home from work. I bleached the siding on my house every year.

I painted a house I lived in for eight years probably six times.

I would do anything to stay in a size five until I was thirty—because that meant I was worthy, right?

I once went through a stage when I brushed my teeth twelve times a day. Yes, the description "OCD" comes to mind, along with many others.

I had a conflict in almost every job I ever had until I was in my late 30s to early 40s. I was always performing for someone, or even against my own false sense of worth.

The truth is there is nothing I could do or get to make myself clean enough, good enough, right enough, skinny enough, pretty enough, smart enough, ANYTHING enough, in my own works. That's because I am only enough in and through the One who made me, and who gave me the very breath I breathe, by the grace of God, through Jesus on the cross, made evident to me by His Holy Spirit. Yet, even in my walk with the Lord, I found myself performing. I was performing for people and for God. I never knew the unconditional love of a father or a mother, or the protection from danger and harm. I thought I had to earn it. My cleaning and order was to have some sort of control over something—a reaction to the chaos going on in my life.

I kept performing. Even when I read my Bible or participated in church, it was about earning. If I read enough, believed enough, prayed enough, or had enough faith, everything would be okay. I was NEVER, EVER enough.

Guess what? That is the truth.

I mentioned this scripture in the last chapter, and it's worth repeating again:

"For it is by grace you have been saved, through faith—and this not from yourselves; it is the gift of God—not by works, so that no one can boast. For we are God's handiwork, created in Christ Jesus to do good works, which God prepared in advance for us to do." (Ephesians 2:8-9)

I have come to the place where I realize that the more I work, the less I have. I was not created for me, but for His glory.

The Apostle Paul summarizes God's supremacy so well in Colossians, chapter 1, verses 15 to 23, when he said: *"The Son is the image of the invisible God, the firstborn over all creation. For in him all things were created: things in heaven and on earth, visible and invisible, whether thrones or powers or rulers or authorities; all things have been created through him and for him. He is before all things, and in him all things hold together. And he is the head of the body, the church; he is the beginning and the firstborn from among the dead, so that in everything he might have the supremacy. For God was pleased to have all his fullness dwell in him, and through him to reconcile to himself all things, whether things on earth or things in heaven, by making peace through his blood, shed on the cross.*

Once you were alienated from God and were enemies in your minds because of your evil behavior. But now he has reconciled you by Christ's physical body through death to present you holy in his sight, without blemish and free from accusation—if you continue in your faith, established and firm, and do not move from the hope held out in the gospel. This is the gospel that you heard and that has been proclaimed to every creature under heaven, and of which I, Paul, have become a servant."

For years, I went to church not really being FREE. I mean free inside—not wearing the outside mask—the one everyone else could see, but God knew better. After all, He is the One who knows all things. He knows about the secret drinking (because wine is "acceptable" in the church). I'd think, "He is a good guy because he goes to church." Or, "They have a Bible study, so it must be okay if they act that way." I had to stop the excuses and get real with myself.

What was the condition of my heart? Was I really more concerned with what religious people thought of me (or any people for that matter), than what the One True Holy God thought?

I began a process of tearing down my false, built-up ideas of religion, and started to develop a relationship with my Abba Father, my Savior Jesus, and the Holy Spirit, my guide and director.

I am still building and refining this relationship, but it is not from a place of performance and work. It has become a place of surrender and acceptance. I have to let go to do this. I have to let go of my expectations, my plans, and how I thought things would be.

I have to accept the hardships and trials as a way to Him, and realize I have to go through those difficulties to get to that new understanding of Him.

Proverbs, chapter 16, verse 9 says, *"A man's heart plans his way, But the Lord directs his steps."*

My plans at the age of thirteen were:

1. To not be my parents

2. To not have kids, so I would not damage another human the way I was; and

3. To kill the pain that I felt

So, I set on a course that led to years of deception, even after I accepted Jesus. I had to come to a place of full surrender, later in life.

CHAPTER SIX

My Plans

I was thirteen years old, and all grown up. I had a job at DQ making a whole $1.50 an hour—enough to pay for my school clothes and personal items. My father didn't pay for "extras."

I seldom saw my mother. She was always moving, or I did not know where she was. She might show up every now and then and maybe take me shopping or have me stay with her at someone's house where she was living. When she did, I was allowed to smoke and drink in front of her.

One time I stayed with her in a basement when she was in between her ex-husbands.

I went out to go wading in the river behind the house, and I fell as I ran from a snake (did I mention I HATE snakes?). I lost my glasses in the river (did I also mention I was legally blind without my glasses?). Well, guess who got into a fight over who should pay for my lost eyeglasses? Yep, my parents. I went months with no glasses because they refused to pay for them. He said "no" because she had me at the time. And she said "no" because she did not have the money. I felt like collateral damage, as most children end up feeling in a divorced home.

Another time, I got hives. I was babysitting and had to go to the emergency room. I could not find either of my parents for a release, and the uncle of the kids I babysat for took me to the hospital.

One of the kids I watched told her uncle I was sixteen, and told me he was twenty-six. I was actually thirteen, and he was thirty. That relationship went on for two-and-a-half years. He would buy me clothes, jewelry, cigarettes, alcohol, and he gave me money. At one point, he went to Missouri for several months and wrote me letters. I didn't date anyone at school and waited for him to move back. I was so brainwashed. However, at the time I had no idea it was actually called grooming and pedophilia. My parents knew it was happening. He stayed in my mom's home overnight on a visit. My dad bought me birth control so I would not get pregnant. After two-and-a-half years, my mother let him come over for Christmas and then threatened to have him eliminated if I did not quit seeing him. I was afraid, so I ended it by going to another relationship that was abusive and unhealthy.

I bounced back and forth between parents. I still had my job—it was the only thing I did have. Then one day, my mother came to my job, walked in, and made me quit on the spot even though I had worked there for over two years. Then she called my dad to come get me, and he said he would have me put in a girls' home if I didn't straighten up. I had basically been taking care of myself since I was nine, and I wasn't going to be told what to do now. I was going to leave home! That was my brilliant plan. And I quit school.

All those events were just more rejections, and again, I felt like I was more collateral damage. I just did not realize at the time that is what my feelings were.

As I am writing this, I realize how amazing, good, and faithful God is. He has brought me through every season and every trial. The enemy came to lie, kill, steal, and destroy, but Jesus came that I might have life and have it to the FULL (or as John 10:10 says, MORE ABUNDANTLY). YES!!!!

He tells us, "Just stay with me. Don't give up!" And He comes with us through every stage, even when we don't realize it. I can't explain it. I don't understand it. But I just need to share this truth.

God is REAL. He IS the Great I AM and worthy of all praise.

I was a walking dead woman, and now I am dead woman, walking alive.

I left home at sixteen for the person who became my daughter's father, and we were together for fifteen years.

We had a marriage ceremony at a courthouse with a false birth certificate he had made that stated I was two years older than I really was, so I could get married. But that technically meant we were not legally married at all.

We ran off to another state, then came back to Tennessee after about three or four months. I needed a place to stay, and my father said, "I have no room for you," even though he had a 2,000-square-foot home.

I know now it was his anger, but to me it was rejection. It was the same rejection I felt when I would tell my dad I loved him as a kid on the phone, and he would say, "Okay. Bye." Then hang up.

You see, I viewed God the same way I viewed my earthly father and mother.

Remember, I never intended to have kids, but I got pregnant five months after running off.

However, I know now that Baby Girl saved my life. I quit every drug and drink and stopped smoking while I was pregnant. I even went to a Bible study with my sister at a lady's house.

I won't ever forget that Spirit-filled, tongue-speaking, hand-laying, and Holy Ghost saturated home. It was the beginning of my long, tumultuous journey with the Father, Son, and Holy Spirit. I was an atheist before that. Even though I had a Bible, I did not believe because of all the things I had been involved with, exposed to, and had done to me.

I accepted Jesus that day and started speaking in tongues. But it was the beginning of a very long journey through the wilderness.

I don't know if you have been through a short season or a long season, if it has been hard, or if it has been light. But no matter what or where you are or have been—He is there.

I love Psalm 139, verses 13 to 16: *For you created my inmost being; you knit me together in my mother's womb. I praise you because I am fearfully and wonderfully made; your works are wonderful, I know that full well. My frame was not hidden from you when I was made in the secret place, when I was woven together in the depths of the earth. Your eyes saw my unformed body; all the days ordained for me were written in your book before one of them came to be.*

Think about that. I mean, really meditate on it.

I started attending a full gospel church, and while I was pregnant, I read my Living Bible every day, sometimes until 3 a.m. I had no phone, no air conditioning, often no car, and I lived in a 12-foot by 57-foot trailer.

After my daughter was born, the nurses asked me if I had gone to the bathroom. I thought they meant where I had been catheterized and said "yes." I had no idea what they meant. So, home I went. Then, with no insurance and scared to tell anyone, I had to use enemas every time to go to the bathroom, and the stool was the size of a pencil and twisted. I was so scared, but I never said a word. I couldn't ask my mother—she never even saw my daughter until Baby Girl was two years old.

I went to the church for a prayer meeting, and the women were all praying in the Spirit in a big circle. I just kind of stood in the meeting, and then I went to get my daughter. But something happened that day. I can still see the lady in my mind today. She had short brown hair, and she walked up to me and laid one hand on my shoulder and one hand on my stomach. She said, "I don't like to do this in public, but the Lord showed me that your intestines were twisted, and He said they will never be twisted again." And ever since then, any time I have had any illness with my stomach, the enemy has tried to tell me, "I thought God healed you!" And I say right back to him, "He did! He said my intestines will never be twisted again, and they are not." I knew then that the God of the Bible that I was reading was truly the God who was real, and I could trust Him. Even though many times I have stumbled and fallen, He has been faithful and still is. That was thirty-eight years ago, and He is still healing me today in so many ways.

Although we lived in that trailer park for six years, we had a great neighbor. I went to church with her because our husbands would not go, and I got baptized. That's an event I won't forget. It was in an outside pool filled with COLD water, fifty-six degrees. I was pushed under a second time because all my hair wasn't wet, and I thought he was trying to drown me.

Even though I went to church and tried hard, I ended up with the character flaws of both of my parents. How could it be? How could this happen? I prayed. I repented. I got anointed. I rebuked. I said every prayer and broke every curse and generational curse I knew. I had counseling. I worked really hard and did all the things I thought I was supposed to do. I got rid of things out of my house, and I didn't listen to or watch things I wasn't supposed to. I grew up in a home that was open to the occult, and I did not want any part of it. No Ouija boards, no dark songs, no fortune telling, no horror movies, no horoscopes, no incense, no pictures or statues that I felt didn't belong. I anointed every home where I lived.

What I did not understand was that I lived in a totally fractured, fallen world. We, as humans, are hurting and broken—and the world we live in is, too. But the redemption of Christ is freely given and received, accepted and surrendered to. It is not earned, or deserved, or something I can just "go get" if I try hard enough. I must fully become humble and surrender to Him. I need to accept HIS will, whatever it may be. I have to walk in forgiveness and repentance.

It is not up to ME. It is all through, and for, and by HIM. I want to know His voice now. I want to follow His lead. I want to love for His sake. My plans are not His plans, because God's ways are not like a man's ways. He is far above me.

I spent fifteen years with my daughter's father. They were very hard years, with multiple times of unfaithfulness. There was also abuse—emotional, physical, sexual, and financial. He would choke me. He would have horrific fits of rage and drive the car 120 miles an hour recklessly, with me and my daughter in the car. When I would scream to stop, he would go faster.

He would take the spark plug wires from under the hood and leave, so I would have no way to drive.

He ran into my car with his truck once with my daughter in it, because I turned the wrong way.

My daughter was so terrified she would wet her pants. There were times he would pull guns on me and others, in front of her.

Our home was a time bomb, and we walked on eggshells. If he ran out of cigarettes, it was my fault. If he ran out of tea, it was my fault. He knew we didn't have money for him to eat out for lunch. So, he would threaten me that if I didn't pack lunch, he would spend the money that was for our bills.

I often worked two or three jobs, carried our insurance, and took care of the house, the yard work, our daughter, and paid the bills.

Once I was able to make enough money to support myself and my daughter, I filed a restraining order, due to his violent nature and the threats on my life. Then I left.

Unfortunately, this led to more bad choices on my part, at the age of thirty-one. I made enough to support us financially, but not emotionally or spiritually. I lived in fear of everything, and I did not even realize it.

Never say "never." I completely stopped drinking for about seven years, except about two times that I recall. I remember the one drink that led me to the next eleven years of drinking, and along with that came a whole host of other horrible choices.

CHAPTER SEVEN

Choices

What did I do? I was divorced, just like my parents. I had moved my daughter three times. Oh no. My mom moved me eight times those first two years after she left my dad. I began to drink nonstop to cover up my pain and my shame, because I had become what I said I would never be. I was living in full-blown sin.

I remember thinking, "What am I doing? This is wrong. I am going to die, and I am going to go to Hell. God really does hate me. He can never forgive me. I can't ever tell anyone. I have to keep my job now, because I can't go to anyone in my family for help. I can't go back to my daughter's father. He will literally kill me. I have nowhere to go. And now God hates me." I had never been so miserable in my life.

I was 2,000 miles from home on a business trip to support my kid. I had to keep the job or we would go hungry and lose our home, and she needed clothes. I couldn't let that happen—I would really be a bad parent then. I got the flu and decided to cancel the second half of my trip and came home. My boss got angry and threatened to fire me from my job. I lay in my bed and told God, "If I lose everything—my job, my home, my kid—I just want You back. I can't be away from You anymore."

It was like the Israelites in the wilderness. They cried out to God, over and over, and He rescued them. I am in no way recommending this type of living. It is not a safe place to be, so close to the edge, to see if He will rescue you. It's not wise to have the mentality of, "Well, I wonder just how close to the edge I can get?" If you are thinking that way, you are already too close.

I got back to church. I quit that job and unfortunately made another bad choice: I met a man in church and got married three months later. He had to be okay; he was in church, right?

Wrong. Now I realize, in my maturation process (and that it is a process), when we are running, we typically run from something and end up running to the very thing we are running from. It just comes dressed up in a different suit.

That marriage lasted five-and-a-half years. It was ravaged in rage, and alcohol, and control that I had never known before. He pulled guns on me—reminders of the stepfather I grew up with and my ex-husband. He disrespected my daughter and me. But we went to church, and we tithed, and he was even on the board. I had a real problem with all of that. I think it's called a "whitewashed tomb."

So, I had another restraining order, and another divorce—more consequences from my choices again.

Once again, I found myself running from something, trying to get to something I had been reading about in my Bible and hearing about for years. But I was still struggling with my own alcohol addiction, the death of my brother from his addiction, and the struggle of reconciling my relationship with my family. I found myself praying, "How do I do this, Lord? You are real. You are faithful. Why am I still so broken and everyone else is so fixed?"

Thank God, during this time He gave me the beginning of a family I did not know I could have: A God-given mom and dad who have stood by me for the past eighteen years. They taught me what family looks like, and does, and teaches, and lives, and loves.

My grandfather's property near Lancaster, Ohio—always a safe place.

We rode in this jeep around my grandfather's property near Lancaster, Ohio. I was thrilled to return to take a picture with it.

This picture shows a good example of my attitude in my 20s.

Introducing my daughter to my grandmother. I was seventeen.

My daughter's first time meeting my grandparents.
We met in a park in Lancaster, Ohio.

"I know I look cute, I may kill you with this gun on the floor."
This is me at age two.

Mark and me on my fortieth birthday.

My cousin, my brother, me, and my sister on my fifth birthday at my grandparents' cabin in California.

Brenda, me, and Kathy at my wedding to Mark.

*Me, my brother, and my sister all ready
for the county fair in Lancaster, Ohio.*

My brother, me, and my sister went to my grandmother's for a big outing: Coat shopping at Goodwill! I remember loving it! I was about five.

Mark and me praying at our wedding.

Me in ninth grade in 1983.

I was five years old and ready for a school play.

My brother, me, my sister, and my Grandma Bernice (Grandma B.) at her house. I was always happy when I was with her.

Gathering to pray at a Celebrate Recovery Summit in 2017.

CHAPTER EIGHT

I Am Still Broken

After finding myself divorced, once again, I wondered how I could be forgiven. For the first time in my life, I was determined to live on my own. I was forty years old, and I was determined to live alone and seek God.

Then a man named Mark began to pursue me relentlessly. He was nothing like what I had ever been. He came from a totally different world, but he had his own hurts and issues (I now see we all do—everyone else really isn't fixed!).

His world was Mayberry RFD. Mine was "no berries for any."

Here's an example: My sister and I told him a story about having to sell Christmas trees one year for money. They were cedar trees, so technically they were not really Christmas trees. He said, "Oh! What troop were you with?" We burst out laughing. He thought we were with a Girl Scout troop, but we were selling trees to feed our family. If we had been smart enough to think of that approach, maybe we could have earned more money, and would not have been so embarrassed standing by the fire barrel while everyone in town drove by.

I am now so grateful Mark stayed persistent, regardless of all the trials and differences, because of all the goodness of the Lord through the working out. (By the way, my God mom and dad—who I met through another very special friend who is no longer here with us—introduced me to Mark, the man who would not stop pursuing me.)

When I bought a condo, Mark was my mortgage lender, and after eighteen months, he became my husband. (I joke that he liked me for my credit scores.) We've now been married for fifteen years.

He was the first man I was honored to go through extensive marriage counseling with. We also honored the Lord with abstinence before marriage—a first for me. You are never too old, and it's never too late!

We have gone through *Celebrate Recovery* together and are now working on twelve years of sobriety together. Over the past fifteen years, we have walked through health, grief, financial disasters, and separation that have almost destroyed us. But these have chiseled, molded, formed, and healed us more and more to who He (God) needs us to be.

I will start with the health side of things and then move to the rest. These are struggles that touch all our lives, in one way or another. Trauma is a real thing. I used to think that I just had a dysfunctional childhood. However, I now realize it was fraught with chaos, confusion, and abuse. Know this: God is and will always be sovereign over all. We have to go *through* to get *to* where He is taking us. When you don't think you can take another day, or another moment, take a deep breath and know you CAN. With Him ALL things are possible (Philippians 4:13).

When Jesus took the road to Golgotha, it was paved with grave pain, and leading up to it was greater suffering than we will ever know. The disciples lay down their lives for the gospel to be carried to the ends of the earth. There is an eternity to be gained, far beyond this earthly body. Oh, what a day it will be!

So, remember when I said God healed me way back in 1985, at that full gospel church, when my intestines were twisted? Well, for most of my life, from the time I was about four years old, I was always sick. I had ear surgeries, ear tubes twice, my tonsils removed, and two mastoidectomies on my right ear. I could not use a public bathroom, and I probably had to go to about eight or nine different gastroenterologists. I had been put on multiple medications. I struggled with eating disorders. I was told I had IBS. I was told my whole life that it was my fault that I was sick. I had multiple female organ problems. At thirty-one, I had to have a hysterectomy.

In 2004, I ended up in the hospital in excruciating pain with a naso-gastric tube because of a blockage, and I was there for seven days. At that time, I was with my second husband, who dropped me off and left me. He did not even tell my daughter I was there. The doctor had to go in and remove scar tissue that was wrapped around my intestines, and he said he had never seen anyone's intestines spread out the way mine were—from the bottom up to the top. At that moment, I knew that was the way God untangled my twisted intestines in 1985. So, every time I was sick, and the enemy would say, "I thought God healed you," I responded, "He said they would never be twisted again." And they were not.

Fast forward to 2008. Mark and I were married, and he knew I had issues with my stomach, but he did not know how bad. I was traveling and got really sick. I called him to pray for me that I would make it home. Over the years, I literally had to use multiple bottles of magnesium citrate in a week just to go. I tried every healthy diet, clean eating, Metamucil—you name it, I did it. I stood on the Word of God, literally with my feet, in the hotel of the Joyce Meyer conference, believing for my healing. Once I had a doctor who had me do ten enemas at one time.

I didn't understand what I had done to deserve this. Again, my whole life I had been told it was my fault. Mark and I went to a new gastroenterologist— I believe it was my eighth or ninth. We had some tests done, and the result was that I had to have my entire colon removed, just a couple years after we were married. This surgery led to a fourteen-day stay in the hospital and another two surgeries.

I was in ICU, and I ended up with a temporary ileostomy, a port, and I was out of work for three months. I went back and had another surgery to have a reconnection.

I tried to live that way for two years and had to run to the bathroom about twenty-five times a day. That did not work well. I had to go back for another surgery two years later, in 2013, and when I had that surgery, they found that my bladder was also holding two liters of fluid. I had to schedule another surgery to have a pacemaker inserted in my sacral nerve in my back so my bladder would function and keep me from having another bag attached for my bladder.

Then, I had to have a permanent ileostomy, which led to another seven days in the hospital. Then, a separate surgery for the pacemaker, which ended up being two surgeries for the pacemaker. The first one left me with wires hanging out my back for two weeks, to make sure that it worked. The second surgery was to go back and have the permanent pacemaker put in.

In 2015, I had to go back to the colorectal doctor and have my ileostomy revised because it was prolapsing, and I had a hernia, and my rectum had to be removed. That was another fourteen-day stay in the hospital, and that trip I almost didn't make it. Actually, with each one of these I almost haven't made it.

In the midst of all of these, I had four knee surgeries,

a nasal and ear surgery, three more bladder surgeries, and three PICC lines. Through this process, I have gradually lost my ability to eat. The food list has gotten smaller and smaller, until recently when I ended up with gastroparesis. They put me on some medication to try and help that, but it didn't work.

In 2022, I got a GJ (gastrojejonostomy) tube, and they tried to feed me through my stomach directly. But that tube would not heal, and it did not work. They had to pull it. I lost thirty-five pounds, and they ended up giving me a PICC line in my left arm, which got a blood clot after six weeks. So, I got a new one in my right arm, and now I live with a TPN for feeding and have been on that for over a year now. I can drink straight liquids only. I have a home health nurse come every Monday and draw my blood. I have a wonderful pharmacist, and I have been able to put on about ten pounds. It's not easy, but God has sustained me, and through all of this He has brought healing to me.

When we think about healing, I often ponder that we think in terms of the outer appearance, the outer man. But we are actually dealing with a spiritual being and realm. Our spirits and our eternities are far greater than the mere flesh and short span that we spend in time, in comparison with eternity.

"If your hand causes you to sin, cut it off. It is better for you to enter into life maimed, rather than having two hands, to go to hell, into the fire that shall never be

quenched—where 'Their worm does not die And the fire is not quenched.'" (Mark 9:43-44 NKJV)

CHAPTER NINE

Don't Let the Makeup and Jewelry Fool You

My life has been full of financial opportunities and trials. One of the things I did as a young person was take things. When I got sober, did my 12 steps, and made amends, part of that healing was to pay back what I had taken. I went all the way back to when I was a teenager. I sent money to people from thirty or more years prior, and I read scripture that said if you could not pay back the original owner, pay back the Lord. So I did—I gave to the church. I paid my tithes and offerings. I gave without expecting back.

I also had to learn that I had become legalistic about it—ouch! Really? Me, religious?

I wanted to follow all the rules, and if I broke one – bam! To Hell I was going. No grace. If I had no grace, I could give no grace. OUCH!

I grew up in a house where I had to earn everything

I got, and nothing was given—NOTHING! The principle was, "You have a roof over your head, so you better help out."

On the other hand – my spouse had it all. That's not wrong, just very different from my experience. We all have a baseline normal. Whatever we grew up with, that's our normal. We don't know anything different. He grew up with a very lucrative life and everything provided—cars, school, sports, a housekeeper, etc.

To bring these two realities together has been a challenge, to say the least. I want to cut back—he wants to make more. I have been a tither (even when I don't live right, I don't want to rob God)—he was not taught that. They were church attenders—I was a heathen who met Jesus, got religious, and tried to earn my way to get God to love me.

After fifteen years, we are now coming together on this. But in the early days of our marriage, he was not open about debt he had, and it came out there were extreme amounts. It caused a lot of distrust in our relationship. It was such a great challenge to overcome, it led to us filing for divorce, selling houses and cars, changing jobs, me moving 2,500 miles away—then God alone reconciling us.

Mark, chapter 10, verse 9 says, *"Therefore what God has joined together, let no one separate."* We are choosing this verse!

I have been broken beyond broken before the Lord. I chose to pray for my husband, and love him, and pray for him, and ask God to give me a gentle spirit.

The three words I have heard are: "surrender" (everything); "be obedient"; and "I require humility." Thankfully, I received these words one at a time, over the past three years.

It echoes Galatians, chapter 5, verses 22 and 23: *"But the fruit of the Spirit is love, joy, peace, forbearance, kindness, goodness, faithfulness, gentleness and self-control. Against such things there is no law."*

It has not all been easy – but it has been worth it.

Money and opportunities—from the outside, everything looks so wonderful. I believe, to some degree, we all paint that picture. I have always said, "Don't let the makeup and jewelry fool you." To look at me, no one would ever know I was sick. When I put on my clothes, you can't see my bags, and tubes, and machines. I cover it up really well, the fact that I am duct-taped and wired together.

The same can be said for our lives, in general. We drive our cars, buy our homes, go to our jobs, go to church, have our Bible studies, see our friends, make small talk, sometimes we even have our prayer groups. We show up and tell people everything is "fine," when in reality it's not.

We need transparency in order to allow healing to happen. It needs to be in safe places, with safe people, with the holy, reverent Word of God as our guide.

Philippians, chapter 4, verse 8 (KJV) says, *"Finally, brethren, whatsoever things are true, whatsoever things are honest, whatsoever things are just, whatsoever things are pure, whatsoever things are lovely, whatsoever things are of good report; if there be any virtue, and if there be any praise, think on these things."*

Joshua, chapter 1, verse 8 (KJV) tells us, *"This book of the law shall not depart out of thy mouth; but thou shalt meditate therein day and night, that thou mayest observe to do according to all that is written therein: for then thou shalt make thy way prosperous, and then thou shalt have good success."*

We went through three years of marriage counseling, even after getting sober. There was repeated financial infidelity on his part, and for me, that was not safe. I could not get to whole forgiveness, which equaled bitterness. When I moved 2,500 miles away, I found myself alone with God. He could work on me alone and Mark alone, and something happened. I quit looking at the speck of dust in my brother's eye and allowed God to work on the plank in my own.

I got in another 12-step *Celebrate Recovery* program and worked on me with God. I quit looking at my husband.

The Lord asked me to pray for him, and I did every day, even without response—until one day he did respond. Then, after a few months, we reconciled. But we are still a work in progress every day. We have a spending plan now, and we work on that together. We are transparent. We pray together daily, first thing in the morning. We make God a priority, personally and together. Tithing is a priority. Praying is a priority. God's Word is a priority. Christian community is a priority. Accountability is a priority. We encourage one another and pray for one another. We still have challenges. Covid has affected our lives in difficult ways, negatively affecting Mark's health, which is a new thing for us.

But the God I know is faithful, and it is in HIM whom I trust.

Grief was something we didn't know how to feel—neither one of us. I was always a productive, self-sufficient, go-getter, type A, could-do-anything person. As a matter of fact, I have a friend who asked me, "Is there anything that you have not done?"

I worked in warehouses. I waited tables. I could hang drywall. I put heating elements in dryers, gas tanks in jeeps, and electrical outlets in houses. I can lay tile (thanks, Dad!). I can do landscaping. I can paint. I was a recruiter for three different businesses. I was an account manager. I worked at a restaurant (DQ, remember?) as the night closer when I was a teenager. I cleaned houses. I did the paperwork for my ex-husband's business and taxes. I always paid the bills and got the insurance for our household. I raised my daughter. I was a real estate agent. I had my human resources certification. I also have my certification in the level 1 Maryland method for trauma. I also got my R-HYI, R-SSYF, R-TSYF, R- HYI Adaptive, touch certification, leadership training, and twenty hours of training from the Center for Trauma and Embodiment (CFTE). I attended two *Celebrate Recovery* training summits, along with leading and continuing to mentor women.

In my job, I spent about seventy percent of my time traveling. I also used to work out six or seven days a week at the gym. I grieve—because of where my health is, I had to give up all those things. However, I made a conscious choice to surrender them.

So, my grief has been:

- Surrendering life as I knew it

- Losing my mother-in-law, who I cared for

- Letting go of the ideas of what I thought things would look like, and accepting what they actually are

I was always the provider. I was always able to protect myself (so I thought). The Lord showed me that I needed to surrender everything completely, and then become obedient, and then humble myself in the fear of the Lord.

It has been a long journey. I often say it's been a tumultuous road. But it's been so worth it.

Luke, chapter 7, verse 47 (NKJV) says, *"Therefore I say to you, her sins, which are many, are forgiven, for she loved much. But to whom little is forgiven, the same loves little."*

I often say that I was the woman at the well, the woman who was about to be stoned, and Mary Magdalene with the seven spirits that Jesus cast out all wrapped up in one. And He saved me. Even though I grieved who I was, and what I lost, I will rejoice in who He's changed me into. I've been made new. I am a new creation in Christ Jesus. As 2 Corinthians, chapter 5, verse 17 (NLT) says, *"This means that anyone who belongs to Christ has become a new person. The old life is gone; a new life has begun!"*

My surrender has been with greater rewards than losses. I have been able to become ordained as clergy. My husband and I are now certified trainers with *Prepare and Enrich*. We have a weekly prayer group in our home. I have been able to record some devotions online and share my story of recovery and sobriety for HIS glory. I am utilizing all the pieces of my life, which He has woven together, to share with others the story and journey of healing.

I practiced trauma care with individuals, helping them from a Christian perspective, for approximately four years with the training I received.

I was trained at two schools that taught yoga from a Christian perspective—not worshiping any other gods. However, after being there for four years, the Holy Spirit convicted me. I was in the midst of studying to get my therapy license, and He said, "STOP." So I did. I was sure it was His voice—I had prayed about whether it was okay to continue, and "STOP" was His response. I did not do any mantras or eastern practices, and I did not use Sanskrit language. I only used Christian music, and I meditated on scripture. But when He said "STOP," I did. It is not that I did not learn what He needed to teach me, but there are doors that can be opened that we don't need to open. And our actions can cause people to stumble. (People can find scripture to back up either side of this debate about yoga—I have heard and seen both sides. I choose to err on the side of Almighty God, and go with not mixing with any other gods, nor opening any doors for curses in my life.)

Joshua, chapter 23, verse 7 (MSG) says, *"Don't get mixed up with the nations that are still around. Don't so much as speak the names of their gods or swear by them. And by all means don't worship or pray to them."*

I will also refer to 1 Corinthians, chapter 10, verses 14 to 33 (ESV*): Therefore, my beloved, flee from idolatry. I speak as to sensible people; judge for yourselves what I say. The cup of blessing that we bless, is it not a participation in the blood of Christ? The bread that we break, is it not a participation in the body of Christ? Because there is one bread, we who are many are one body,* *for we all partake of the one bread. Consider the people of Israel: are not those who eat the sacrifices participants in the altar? What do I imply then? That food offered to idols is anything, or that an idol is anything? No, I imply that what pagans sacrifice they offer to demons and not to God. I do not want you to be participants with demons. You cannot drink the cup of the Lord and the cup of demons. You cannot partake of the table of the Lord and the table of demons. Shall we provoke the Lord to jealousy? Are we stronger than he?*

"All things are lawful," but not all things are helpful. "All things are lawful," but not all things build up. Let no one seek his own good, but the good of his neighbor. Eat whatever is sold in the meat market without raising any question on the ground of conscience. For "the earth is the Lord's, and the fullness thereof." If one of the unbelievers invites you to dinner and you are disposed to go, eat whatever is set before you without raising any question on the ground of conscience. But if someone says to you, "This has been offered in sacrifice," then do not eat it, for the sake of the one who informed you, and for the sake of conscience—I do not mean your conscience, but his. For why should my liberty be determined by someone else's conscience? If I partake with thankfulness, why am I denounced because of that for which I give thanks?

So, whether you eat or drink, or whatever you do, do all to the glory of God. Give no offense to Jews or to Greeks or to the church of God, just as I try to please everyone in everything I do, not seeking my own advantage, but that of many, that they may be saved.

CHAPTER TEN

Healing: A Short Trip and a Long Journey

The beginning of my journey to healing began around age sixteen. Although there was a lot of pain in the midst, and I was pregnant, I had accepted Christ as my Savior – that was the first step.

I had received the gift of the Holy Spirit, and was able to pray in the Spirit, but I was not free. I had not yet made Jesus the LORD of my life. I did not know how. I did get baptized, but stopped going to church because I got hurt. By the way, our greatest hurts will be there, because church is made up of people just like me and you. Remember the woman who was chased into the street and about to be stoned, and all those men who accused her? Jesus responded by casually drawing a line on the dirt, then said: "Let he who is with no sin cast the first stone at her." They all dropped the stones, and one by one, they walked away. He asked, "Where are your accusers?" She had none, and

He told her to go and sin no more.

In my journey with the Lord, I read my Bible. I prayed. I watched Joyce Meyer. I taught a Sunday school class. I stayed married, even though it was abusive, for fifteen years. I did anything and everything (in my mind) to be good. Key words: in MY mind.

At the age of twenty-three, I had a breakdown and eating disorders, and I signed myself into Middle Tennessee Christian Hospital. It was my first real exposure to counseling. After a week, they allowed me to go home. I had outpatient counseling twice per week for a few months. This began a long process of unlayering my life.

I started exercising more instead of eating / binging or restriction. I ate healthy food so I would be good. I renounced evil, had others walk through deliverance with me, went through recovery, walked through the steps to freedom in Christ, dug deep into Christ-centered counseling, inner healing, EMDR therapy, became certified in multiple trauma centered body modalities, and Murray Method trauma healing. The Lord literally taught me, and still is daily walking me through, to get to healing. We can't give away what we don't have.

Something I have come to say, as of late, is that I am "claying it out." Not fleshing it out. Because He is the potter, and I am the clay. When I say, "Dig deep and be clay," I should probably take a moment to elaborate a bit on what that actually looks like.

I had so much anger in me from being dismissed, betrayed, violated, and let down. I actually chased a man down with my car and got out and yelled at him for giving me the one finger. I was maybe twenty-three and 118 pounds (and stupid, I might add). I could not hug anyone—male or female—until I was in my 40s. I could not be touched without flinching and wanting to punch someone. I didn't believe anyone, or trust anyone, including myself— because of the level of deception I had lived in, and the bad choices I had made as a result. It took years of work and surrendering to Christ, and I am still one-day-at-a-time surrendering to Him, asking, "What is there in me that needs to go that I might get closer to You, Lord? If there is anything, please show it to me, and forgive me of my sins, for I know they have been many."

Recently, several people have said something to me, and their statements led to healing. Here are a few examples:

At a counseling appointment, I realized it was okay to do the things I needed to do to be obedient to the Lord. My counselor responded, "No, it is not just okay. It is healthy." WOW! I have never been told I was healthy before. Healthy! I really had to think about that, and I have been writing that down about myself for several weeks.

My husband recently said to me, "I used to think I just got the leftover remains of you, and now I realize that I got the best parts of you." Yes, I am crying. How wonderful is that? You can't get that unless you are broken.

You know, Paul asked God to heal him three times, and God replied that His grace was sufficient. But I think we overlook that the previous verses, 2 Corinthians, chapter 12, verses 6 to 9 say, *"... so no one will think more of me than is warranted by what I do or say, or because of these surpassingly great revelations. Therefore, in order to keep me from becoming conceited, I was given a thorn in my flesh, a messenger of Satan, to torment me. Three times I pleaded with the Lord to take it away from me. But he said to me, 'My grace is sufficient for you, for my power is made perfect in weakness.' Therefore I will boast all the more gladly about my weaknesses, so that Christ's power may rest on me."*

The Lord showed me that, as of this month, I have been sober twelve years—and not only that, but it is the longest period of time in my life that I have ever been sober, and I am fifty-five years old. It was an epiphany for me. I was able to see the reality of not drinking for twelve years, and take in that I was experiencing the longest time I had ever been sober.

A prayer that helped me on my recovery journey is the serenity prayer—I think you'll enjoy reading the full version:

God, grant me the serenity to accept the things I cannot

change, the courage to change the things I can, and the wisdom to know the difference, living one day at a time; enjoying one moment at a time; taking this world as it is, not as I would have it; Trusting You will make all things right if I surrender to Your will; So that I may be reasonably happy in this life and supremely happy with You forever in the next. — Reinhold Niebuhr

I stopped drinking and crawled, fell, stumbled, and finally walked (and am still walking!) the hard Recovery Road, and there is no way to go into all the details of every aspect—but God!

During this time of sobriety, He has been sustaining me on a PICC line and through multiple surgeries that brought me close to death.

I'd like to share some of my trauma and healing modalities that have helped me in my journey (I often say I am held together with duct tape and wires—and sustained by Jesus). They have helped me in my healing journey, as I call the hard, holy work. I pray in some way it can help others see the power of a Risen Savior who comes to walk with us and be in the messiness with us. He did not come and suffer to take it all away, but to show us how to walk out the trials and messiness with grace, mercy, and compassion, which we can then bestow on others.

The Lord's prayer: *Our Father who art in heaven, Hallowed be thy Name. Thy kingdom come. Thy will be done, On earth as it is in heaven. Give us this day our daily bread. And forgive us our trespasses, As we forgive those who trespass against us. And lead us not into temptation, But deliver us from evil. [For thine is the kingdom, and the power, and the glory, for ever and ever.]* (Matthew 6:9-13)

I often contemplate the statement, "As we forgive those who trespass against us." Did you know we will be forgiven in the same manner that we forgive?

Matthew, chapter 6, verses 14 and 15 say, *"For if you forgive other people when they sin against you, your heavenly Father will also forgive you. But if you do not forgive others for their sins, your Father will not forgive your sins."*

Whoa!! Did you get that? It's not about if they DESERVE it, if they EARNED it, or if we FEEL like it—forgiveness is a CHOICE to honor the Lord, the Creator of the universe. He forgives us first, that we might forgive. Amen.

This truth has been a big part of healing for me. I have had to choose to forgive many things, on a daily basis.

CHAPTER ELEVEN

Healing Roads

Many roads can lead you home, but only one can lead you to the eternal Kingdom, and that is Jesus Christ, the King of kings. John, chapter 14, verse 6 says, *"Jesus answered, 'I am the way and the truth and the life. No one comes to the Father except through me.'"*

I want to start there, because that is where He started with me. As I lie down each night and wake each morning, it is He who enables me. He provides the roof over my head, the water in my faucet, and the pillow under my head. Only by His great grace and mercy am I saved and sustained.

His Word is life to me.

John, chapter 1, verses 1 to 5 say, *"In the beginning was the Word, and the Word was with God, and the Word was God. He was with God in the beginning. Through Him all things were made; without Him nothing was made that has been made. In Him was life, and that life was the light of all mankind. The light shines in the darkness, and the darkness has not overcome it."*

Then verse 14 says, *"The Word became Flesh and made His dwelling among us. We have seen His glory, the glory of the one and only Son, who came from the Father, full of grace and truth."*

These are probably two of my favorite verses. Here are some more:

In the beginning God created the heavens and the earth. (Genesis 1:1)

So God created Mankind in His own image, in the image of God He created them; male and female He created them. (Genesis 1:27)

Then the Lord God formed a man from the dust of the ground and breathed into his nostrils the breath of life, and the man became a living being. (Genesis 2:7)

The Hebrew definition of that breath is the Spirit breath, "Ruach HaKodesh," which means comforter, breath, or wind.

There are so many people, places, challenges, and opportunities that the Lord has used to continue the work He started. And to think it began long before I was ever born! According to Jeremiah, chapter 1, verse 5, *"Before I formed you in the womb I knew you, before you were born I set you apart; I appointed you as a prophet to the nations."*

Psalm 139, verse 16 (ESV) says, *"Your eyes saw my unformed substance; in your book were written, every one of them, the days that were formed for me, when as yet there was none of them."*

Job, chapter 31, verse 15 (ESV) tells us, *"Did not he who made me in the womb make him? And did not one fashion us in the womb?"*

Isaiah, chapter 44, verse 2 (ESV) says, *"Thus says the Lord who made you, who formed you from the womb and will help you: Fear not, O Jacob my servant, Jeshurun whom I have chosen."*

These are just a few scriptures that refer to the Lord creating and knowing us before we existed. It's a powerful thought, that the Creator of All Things would know me.

Every part of me is known. The very breath in my lungs is the breath from and of God. Every inhale and exhale. His Word is life.

In Deuteronomy, chapter 30, verse 19 (ESV), He said: *"I call heaven and earth as witnesses against you today, that I have set before you life and death, blessing and curse. Therefore choose life, that you and your offspring may live..."*

I began to speak the Word of God out loud over my life. I don't mean in a health, wealth, and prosperity way. I mean in a "Lord, help me break free from this place I am in" kind of way.

I read, and I read A LOT.

I watched Joyce Meyer almost every morning for probably twenty years and attended her conferences in Missouri three or four times. I wrote scripture, and I journaled. I wrote with colored pencils and pens in notebooks, 3x5 index cards, sticky notes, and on color-coded cards to help me remember. I listened to only Christian music or worship songs. One by one, God began to tear down the strongholds in my life.

Keep in mind, I came from a background of not only abandonment, but rejection, physical, emotional, and sexual abuse, and an unhealthy view of God. My old structures had to be dismantled so God could create in me a clean heart (Psalm 51).

I found old journals from 2008 that I had written proclamations in:

I will be a respectful, godly wife.

My husband will serve the Lord and lead us.

We will be out of debt.

Our cars will be paid in full.

We owe no man a debt but a debt of love.

As I read through that, I realized so much of what I

prayed for, and stood on faith for, has come to pass—all amongst the turmoil of life, loss, separation, surgery after surgery, financial plummets, dishonesty, and walking out sobriety. All of it! In the MIDST, He is right there—just like He was in the boat with the disciples in the MIDST of the storm. He doesn't always take away the storm, trauma, heartache, or loss, but He does offer to be with us, and He uses all things for good.

As Romans chapter 8, verse 28 says, *"And we know that in all things God works for the good of those who love him, who have been called according to his purpose."*

I want to make sure to communicate that healing oftentimes looks different than what we may think or want it to. Or maybe it comes to us in a different delivery than we anticipate. Yet, it comes, nonetheless. And for that, I praise Him and give Him glory and thanksgiving, honor and praise.

At this point, I would like to share a list of some of the books I have read over the years that have helped me in my journey to healing. It is a pretty long list, but not exhaustive.

The number one top seller on my list is the Bible. You can choose your translation; just get it, read it, then read it again, and again, and again, and again, and again. Each time, ask the Lord to read YOU. It WILL transform you. As Curt Thompson writes, "One reason many people find

Scripture to be so regenerative is that, fundamentally, it is a story—one told by many different voices. All of its authors were confronted by a Person. In the course of that encounter, whether it lasted a moment or over a lifetime, each storyteller was changed by that other Voice. He or she was transformed by a God (who would not be limited by left-brain, logical, linear theology) who in the beginning got his hands dirty in the soil of creation and later got them bloodied in the agony and beauty of redemption." (*Anatomy of the Soul* by Curt Thompson, page 81)

I am not who I need to be, but I am not who I used to be, and He is not done with me yet! I don't plan to stop reading until I am no longer alive.

Here are some more books I highly recommend:

The Power of Proclamation, Derek Prince

New Morning Mercies, Paul David Tripp

The Choice, Dr. Edith Eva Edgar

A Prisoner of Another War, Marilyn Murray

Red Sea Rules, Robert Morgan

SOZO, Dawna Desilva and Teresa Liebsher

The Forgotten Way, Ted Dekker

Big Trouble Ahead, Allen Jackson

Do It Afraid, Joyce Meyer

The Steps to Freedom in Christ, Neil T. Anderson

Fierce Conversations, Susan Scott

Eat This Book, Eugene Peterson

Hand Me Another Brick, Charles Swindoll

Boundaries, Henry Cloud and John Townsend

Embodied Prayer, Celeste Snowber

The Soul of Shame, Curt Thompson

Anatomy of the Soul, Curt Thompson

The Awe of God, John Bevere

The Body Keeps the Score, Besser van der Kolk

Suffering and the Heart of God, Diane Langberg

Screwtape Letters, C.S. Lewis

Bonhoeffer, Eric Metaxas

Letter to the American Church, Eric Metaxas

Right-Brained Child in a Left-Brained World, Jeffrey Freed and Laurie Parsons

I spent a lot of time reading as an adult, but I did not have that investment as a child. I learned that I was dyslexic much later in life. However, by reading so much and using the tools of color coding, it assisted me. I found that I actually LOVED learning history, science, and the deep stuff of God and what He does, even when I don't understand it. Because He is God, and I don't have to understand it to appreciate and believe it. I am in awe of HIM.

Another key to my healing was starting *Celebrate Recovery* and working the program. We say, "It works if you work it," and EVERYONE has a hurt, a habit, or a hang up. I believe we all need the cleansing, redeeming blood of Jesus to bring us back into a right relationship with the Father. I had to take an honest inventory of my life, my character, who I thought I was, and who I really was.

It was also tremendously helpful to begin therapy with a Christian counselor I trust. I did whatever homework they assigned. If they suggested I should make amends with someone, I did. If I needed to get art paper and crayons to draw out my feelings, and then mark them out to get rid of the negative thought patterns, I did.

Philippians, chapter 4, verse 8 (ESV) says: *Finally, brothers, whatever is true, whatever is honorable, whatever is just, whatever is pure, whatever is lovely, whatever is commendable, if there is any excellence, if there is anything worthy of praise, think on these things.*

When I needed to choose forgiveness, I chose and still do choose forgiveness.

As I journeyed through healing, my body continued to

deteriorate. I began working with a personal trainer who was a Christian with a private gym. She taught a class for stretching and strengthening without using weights. It was so helpful to me, I wanted to get certified to teach.

I was limited in my movement and in other capacities, and she shared a place that taught from a Christ-centered perspective. My husband and I prayed, I sought counsel, and I went through training and acquired teaching certifications in several body modalities. But the modality I focused on most was trauma movement care. I taught for five years, using Scripture with Christian music. I became certified in level one Murray Method.

My husband and I are now trained to be *Prepare / Enrich* marriage facilitators. That is a big part of our collective healing journey together. We have a heart for marriages and families. I can't begin to describe the level of intimacy, restoration, and humility we both have walked through— and still are!

Sometimes I think about what it would be like to package up all my baggage, hand it to someone, and say, "Here! Just open this and carry it around for a day. See how it feels, and maybe how it affects you emotionally, physically, spiritually, mentally, relationally, and financially." I wonder if the weight would be heavy enough to make a change or an impact on their lives? It might feel like approaching a red, flashing light at a railroad crossing: Danger! Train is coming! STOP!!!

The trauma we experience does leave an imprint, and we need help and space to remove that pain. Sometimes— oftentimes—the trauma that comes to us is not of our own doing, but by the doing of someone else, and we feel as though we are left to gather up the pieces.

BUT GOD!

Mark, chapter 10, verse 27 says, *"Jesus looked at them and said, 'With man this is impossible, but not with God; all things are possible with God.'"*

CHAPTER TWELVE

Embodied Prayer and Healing Movement

The body and movement is also an expression of worship and an expression of healing. When Mary went to visit Elizabeth, John began moving within her womb at the very presence of Mary, who had Jesus within her. He was celebrating the Savior!

King David danced in worship to the Lord, uninhibited.

God breathed His very breath into Adam's nostrils.

Often when we face trauma in our lives, we face the natural-given responses of fight, flight, freeze, or fawn. Now, given a normal circumstance, these are healthy responses. For example, if you were hiking one day in the woods and a big bear came along, you would get scared. The natural response would be to freeze or to take flight! Or maybe you would want to fight!

Now, imagine you are a small child living in a suburb,

and you come home every day to an empty house. There is no food, and you're not sure when the adults will show up. If and when they do come home, will they be sober or drunk? Will they try to get in your room? Will you have clean clothes for school tomorrow? Will you have lunch money? Now you live with the bear, and your natural, God-given response system is stuck in the "on" mode ALL of the time.

We need to work on turning it off. I would like to share some tools to put in your toolbox that I believe are safe, practical, and biblically sound to help unlock the trauma physically, and to help people walk in freedom. (Lord, help us to walk this out, as You have helped me. Because You are faithful.)

I believe the Holy Spirit reveals to each of us what we are ready to process, when we are ready and willing to. We are always a work in process, and it's the old saying that it's like peeling an onion, layer, by layer, by layer. The layers of an onion are very thin. They burn your eyes when you cut them. They stink quite awfully, yet they add so much flavor to so many recipes. If you chop, cut, or slice them with a sharp knife, and toss them in a hot pan with some butter, and sauté them—well then, you have something different altogether. That's a lot like the process for us: peeling one layer at a time, cutting, slicing, chopping, frying in the heat. But the end result is a sweet, caramelized addition to the meal, or a critical ingredient for a wonderful meal.

The Body Keeps the Score by Dr. Bessel van der Kolk is a very hard read, yet full of real and hard-to-digest, true stories. Our current world is full of very hard and real, true, and awful stories.

How do we heal from the brokenness?

How do we still get up when we are left with shattered pieces?

How do we move from the fight, flight, freeze, or fawn response?

What happens to the body, mind, and soul through trauma, scientifically?

God already created a way—in HIS magnificence, omniscience, holiness, and redemptive wonder.

Revelation, chapter 12, verse 11 (NKJV) says, *"And they overcame him by the blood of the Lamb and by of the word of their testimony; and they did not love their lives to the death."*

They did not love their lives and renounce their faith, even when faced with death. They devoted themselves to worship and prayer, to heal what the enemy and adversary of our soul tried to steal and destroy.

John, chapter 10, verses 7 to 10 say, *"Therefore Jesus said again, 'Very truly I tell you, I am the gate for the sheep. All who have come before me are thieves and robbers, but the sheep have not listened to them. I am the gate; whoever enters through me will be saved. They will come in and go out, and find pasture. The thief comes only to steal and kill and destroy; I have come that they may have life, and have it to the full.'"*

Jesus told this simple story, but they had no idea what He was talking about. So, He tried again. Here's my paraphrase: "I'll be explicit, then. I am the gate for the sheep. All those others are up to no good—sheep rustlers, every one of them. But the sheep didn't listen to them. I am the gate. Anyone who goes through me will be cared for. They will freely go in and out, and they will find pasture. A thief is only there to steal, kill, and destroy. I came so they can have real and eternal life—more and better life than they ever dreamed of."

In previous chapters, we've talked about how my journey has been long and tumultuous. In this chapter, I'd like to focus on movement before and with the Lord. Although I may be limited in my physical abilities from life circumstances, I can still move, walk, pray, and worship. In the movement of doing those things, it releases the trauma that has been pinned up. In this way, we work out the pain.

When I focus on the Word, it renews the mind. Romans, chapter 12, verse 2 (ESV) says, *"Do not be conformed to this world, but be transformed by the renewing of your mind, that by testing you may discern what is the will of God, what is good and acceptable and perfect."*

Part of recovering our bodies is accepting our in-between states—our imperfections—and acknowledging that we are clay. I recommend reading *Embodied Prayer: Harmonizing Body and Soul* by Celeste Snowber Schroeder.

We can engage with our whole being—body, mind, and spirit. In 1 Samuel, chapter 16, David was called upon to play music for Saul to bring him relief as he was tormented by an evil spirit. 1 Samuel, chapter 16, verse 23 says, *"Whenever the spirit from God came on Saul, David would take up his lyre and play. Then relief would come to Saul; he would feel better, and the evil spirit would leave him."*

I often listen to worship music and praise God. I have the privilege of getting to participate in intercessory prayer at my local church in the mornings during the week. I have grown to love walking, kneeling, community, and sitting prayer time. There truly is a release, and the only true way to heal is with God. It was already totally integrated into us by HIM. As we give Him praise, He returns healing.

I have tried to integrate many spiritual disciplines into my daily life:

- Morning prayer with my husband and in community

- Daily Bible reading

- Regularly attending Bible studies

- Attending church and serving others

- Weekly home prayer meetings

- Communion

- Worship

- Listening to the Holy Spirit

- Contemplation and meditating on the Word of God. *(The Joy of the Lord! For it is our strength!)*

- Walking and praying

- Breath prayers

- Bowing before the Lord

- Dancing, worshiping, and praying

- Christ-centered counseling

- Practicing thankfulness

All of these require action on my part, but God always meets us. He is always waiting, and never leaves nor forsakes us. But we have a free will to choose to participate in the great adventure!

I believe God gave us the natural ability to work the trauma and pain out of our bodies as we pray, and worship, and sing with thanksgiving to Him. We were made to worship and glorify Him, and when we do what we were created for, there comes a natural healing— just as He made the body to heal.

Think of when you have a cold or a cut. The whole body reacts by rushing white and red blood cells to the area of the body with injury and getting to work. If you are in an accident, your body goes into shock to protect you.

As we continue, you will see how the trauma of life can injure us and get parts of us stuck. But in the God-gifted and God-given breath, movement, and life instructions, we receive healing, freedom, and health in ways we never thought we could.

I would like to stress that we have to accept that His ways are not ours, and that does require humility, obedience, and surrender. Oh, but what rejoicing, glory and praise come with doing those things.

There are days I am so physically exhausted. My voice is weak. I have anemia. I think to myself, "I just don't want to hook up to the PICC line today. I just don't want to _____ (fill in the blank)." Then I catch myself, and I get my thankful pants on and look around me and remember the days of small beginnings. I thank God for all of my medical supplies and that I GET to hook up to a PICC line at home. I GET to have the ileostomy that has kept me alive for the past twelve years. I get to live in a really nice home, drive a nice car, take a hot shower, brush my teeth, wash my clothes at home, have heat and air conditioning, and I have a safe place to come home to. I have a church to worship and pray in that is safe. I could go on...

Then I get in the Word.

Then I go to prayer.

Then I worship.

Sometimes I have appointments with my trusted counsel. Sometimes it's a play day or a couch day. Whatever day it is, I have learned this: Your FEELINGS do not matter, nor are they relevant. I tell my feelings, "You go sit down in the corner, and you don't tell me what to do. I am doing the truth of the Word of God." Then I get my Bible and go find truth. I speak out proclamations and begin moving and worshiping.

Breath prayers are another way to bring movement using your breath. Our very breath comes from God. Genesis, chapter 2, verse 7 says, *"Then the Lord God formed a man from the dust of the ground and breathed into His nostrils the breath of life, and the man became a living creature."*

A breath prayer is a practice of inhaling and exhaling a scripture or prayer, repeating it several times in a row. For example:

Inhale: Be still and know
Exhale: I am God.
Repeat three times.

Inhale: I trust
Exhale: in Jesus.
Repeat three times.

Inhale: I don't have a spirit of fear.

Exhale: I have a Spirit of love, power, and sound mind.

Repeat three times.

2 Corinthians, chapter 1, verses 21 and 22 tell us, *"Now it is God who makes both us and you stand firm in Christ. He anointed us, set his seal of ownership on us, and put his Spirit in our hearts as a deposit, guaranteeing what is to come. "*

I also love the promise of I Peter, chapter 5, verse 7: *"Cast all your anxiety on Him because He cares for you. "*

The joy of the Lord – this too is a choice, I have found, and it really has been a good one for me. I have learned to laugh, and to laugh a lot. I make jokes and don't take things too seriously. I used to take everything seriously. We may not get to choose everything that comes to us, but we can choose our responses.

Please listen to my heart and don't misunderstand me. I still deal with pain. I have struggles and feel sadness, sorrow, grief, and more. But in the midst of all of this, God has given me a quirky sense of humor and an ability to rebound. I like to have fun—the kind of fun that's playful, having the heart of a child (not childish). If there is a statue out somewhere, I will climb it and get my photo. If there is furniture in Costco, I will be the furniture model. I make fake commercials and send them to my daughter and nieces. We pose in front of other people's Christmas decorations in their yards for photo ops. I am quick-witted, yet the Lord has had to correct me in this, so that my wit is not sarcasm.

Do I still have work to do? Sure! Along with surrendering, humility, obedience, and working out my salvation with fear and trembling.

2 Corinthians, chapter 1, verses 21 to 23 say, *"And it is God who establishes us with you in Christ, and has anointed us, and who has also put his seal on us and given us his Spirit in our hearts as a guarantee. But I call God to witness against me—it was to spare you that I refrained from coming again to Corinth."*

My hope and my prayer is that the journey of life, which God has graced me with, will help others find healing through the Word of God—for His Word is life, and it is the well that never runs dry.

Conclusion

I was born in Columbus, Ohio, and lived my toddler and young years near Dayton, Ohio. Truly, my most tender memories took place during that time, even though they had hidden terror in them. I believe all stories do. No one gets to go through this side of life unscathed.

I also believe those difficulties are what builds, molds, matures, and creates us to be who we are truly meant to be. We have to shed all the worldly off of us. What the enemy means for harm, God uses for His good. Remember Romans, chapter 8, verse 28: *"And we know that all things work together for good to them that love God, to them who are the called according to his purpose."*

As I have shared my story with you and left a few of the tools that have helped me, I am praying it will, in some way, encourage you to keep going. Know that God is the Creator of the universe, and that He truly does love us. He is coming back for His Church, and we get to participate in the greatest adventure on planet Earth.

What will we choose? Will we allow the hard things in life to build our character and resolve, or will they break us? I think sometimes they can do both. It's not "either / or," it's "and."

Psalm 23

The Lord is my shepherd, I lack nothing.

He makes me lie down in green pastures,

he leads me beside quiet waters,

he refreshes my soul.

He guides me along the right paths

for his name's sake.

Even though I walk

through the darkest valley,

I will fear no evil,

for you are with me;

your rod and your staff,

they comfort me.

You prepare a table before me

in the presence of my enemies.

You anoint my head with oil;

my cup overflows.

Surely your goodness and love will follow me

all the days of my life,

and I will dwell in the house of the Lord

forever.

Now I am entering a new season of this journey of life. The following verse from Matthew has become a staple in my daily thoughts and meditations:

"If anyone causes one of these little ones—those who believe in me—to stumble, it would be better for them to have a large millstone hung around their neck and to be drowned in the depths of the sea. Woe to the world because of the things that cause people to stumble! Such things must come, but woe to the person through whom they come! If your hand or your foot causes you to stumble, cut it off and throw it away. It is better for you to enter life maimed or crippled than to have two hands or two feet and be thrown into eternal fire. And if your eye causes you to stumble, gouge it out and throw it away. It is better for you to enter life with one eye than to have two eyes and be thrown into the fire of hell." (Matthew 18:6-9, emphasis added)

The phrase "to enter life" caused me to pause. I am stepping into eternity. It's a perspective, a choice. The Lord tells us in His Word that He lays before us life and death, blessings and curses. Choose life.

I made a decision a long time ago, when the doctor told me my life span may be cut a bit short, that I will go out living!

I choose Jesus as Lord. I choose Him now!

I choose joy!

I choose forgiveness, repeatedly.

I choose the Truth.

Each day when I wake up is a new day that I get to choose.

Do I always feel like it? No. Does my body still want to cooperate? No. But I have, and I am. Every day I am praising Him and thanking Him for every good and perfect gift, as they are from Him.

So, as my wonderful counselor says when ask her, "How long will it take? How long will I need to work on this?"

She so gently responds, "Until ..."

We often get stuck in wanting to know the results, the end of the story. Here are my conclusions:

1. The results are up to the Holy Spirit.

2. Only God knows the heart of a man.

3. Better to get the plank out of my own eye than look for the speck in my brother's.

4. It's not "what's wrong" with someone. The question really is: "What happened to them?"

5. In order to get to healing, you MUST go through the pain.

Helpful Prayers and Affirmations

Prayer of Salvation

Lord Jesus Christ,

I believe You are the Son of God and the only way to God.

I believe that Jesus died on the cross for my sins.

I am a sinner. I need a Savior.

I repent of all my sins and ask You to come into my heart.

I believe that You do forgive me.

I also forgive all who have sinned against me.

This day I choose to make You Lord of my Life.

In Jesus' name, amen.

(from World Outreach Church, Murfreesboro, Tennessee, wochurch.org)

Prayer of Forgiveness

Lord, I forgive_____for _____.
I take authority over the enemy, and in the name of Jesus
Christ and by the power of His Holy Spirit, I take back the
ground I have allowed Satan to gain in my life, because
of my attitude toward _____, and I give this
ground back to my Lord Jesus Christ.
(from World Outreach Church, Murfreesboro, Tennessee, wochurch.org)

By the Blood of the Lamb and the Word of My Testimony, I Overcome the Devil!

Revelation 12:11: *They triumphed over him by the blood
of the lamb and the word of their testimony; they did not
love their lives so much as to shrink from death.*

Through the blood of Jesus, I am redeemed out of the
hand of the devil.

Through the blood of Jesus, all of my sins are forgiven.

The blood of Jesus Christ, God's Son, continually
cleanses me from all sin.

Through the blood of Jesus, I am justified, made
righteous, just as if I'd never sinned.

Through the blood of Jesus, I am sanctified, made holy,
set apart to God.

My body is a temple of the Holy Spirit: Redeemed,
cleansed, sanctified by the blood of Jesus.

Therefore, because of all that's gone before, Satan has no

place in me and no power over me.

Through the blood of Jesus Christ,

I renounce him, loose myself from him, and command him to leave me in the name of Jesus.

(from Derek Prince Ministries, derekprince.com)

The Apostles' Creed

I believe in God, the Father Almighty, Maker of Heaven and Earth. And in Jesus Christ, His only Son, our Lord; Who was conceived by the Holy Spirit, born of the Virgin Mary, suffered under Pontius Pilate, was crucified, died, and was buried. He descended into Hades; the third day He rose again from the dead: He ascended into Heaven, and sits at the right hand of God, the Father Almighty; from thence He shall come to judge the living and the dead. I believe in the Holy Spirit, the holy Christian Church, the communion of saints, the forgiveness of sins, the resurrection of the body, and the life everlasting. Amen.

The Lord's Prayer

Our Father which art in heaven, Hallowed be thy name. Thy kingdom come, Thy will be done in earth, as it is in heaven. Give us this day our daily bread. And forgive us our debts, as we forgive our debtors. And lead us not into temptation, but deliver us from evil: For thine is the kingdom, and the power, and the glory, for ever. Amen.
(Matthew 6:9-13 KJV)

The Knot Prayer (author unknown)

Dear God –

Please untie the knots that are in my mind, my heart, and my life. Remove the have nots, can nots, and the do nots. Erase the will nots, the may nots, and might nots that may find a home in my heart. Release me from the could nots, would nots, and should nots that obstruct my life. And most of all, dear God, I ask You remove from my mind, my heart, And my life, all of the am nots that I have allowed to hold me back.Especially the thought that I am not good enough.

Amen

Daily Proclamation and Thanksgiving Before the Lord

I thank You that You will create in me a clean heart, oh God, and renew a steadfast spirit within me, and not remove Your Holy Spirit from me.

I thank You that I delight myself in You, Lord, and You give me the desires of my heart.

I thank You I am fearfully and wonderfully made.

I thank You I am more than a conqueror in Christ Jesus.

I thank You that You will complete the work You started in me and my entire family.

I thank You that I am in a covenant relationship with You, with my husband, and Your Church, and that NOTHING can separate me from Your love.

I thank You that I am a good listener, and that I walk and live by the fruit of the Spirit.

I thank You that I walk in love, mercy, and forgiveness, and extend grace to others and myself, as You have extended and covered me.

I thank You that I am a good steward over the time, talents, and gifts You have given me, as they are all from You, to You, and for Your glory,

I thank You that I can do all things through Christ Jesus, and that with man it may be impossible, but with God all things are possible.

I thank You that there is no weapon formed against me that will prosper.

I thank You that there is no suffering in this present time or flesh that compares to the glory that is to come.

I thank You that You are my hope and salvation.

I thank You that You are my shield and my guard, and that You will walk through the valley of the shadow of death with me.

I thank You that Your wings cover me and that though a thousand may fall at my side and ten thousand at my right hand, the plagues will not come near me.

I thank You that all of our children serve the Lord with joy, and that You have completed the great work You started in each of them.

I thank You that You are healing to my soul and spirit, and as it prospers, so does my body.

I thank You that I shall not die, but I shall live and proclaim the works of the Lord.

I thank You that, as for me and my house, we serve the Lord.

I thank You that I am good in health, even as my soul prospers.

I thank You that I speak life and truth, for as a man thinks and speaks, he is.

I thank You that we are debt free, for we owe no man a debt but the debt of love.

I thank You that we serve the Kingdom of Heaven for eternity for You, Father, Son, and Holy Spirit.

I thank You that we can enter into worship with all of Heaven and creation, and sing, "Holy, Holy, Holy, is the Lord God Almighty. For the lamb who was slain."

I thank You that I am precious in Your sight, and that I am daily in the undoing and becoming what You created me to be.

I thank You I am Your daughter—loved, cherished, and precious, and I do not have to perform for anyone.

(by Cheryl Hollinshead)

Helpful Videos

Visit my YouTube channel to find a few videos that build upon everything you've read in this book.

One video was filmed by Branches, my counseling center for over twelve years. I recorded a testimony to share the many ways they helped me find freedom and healing.

The second is called "Healing Through the Word and Movement." It contains more of my story and how I've found healing through God's Word, worship, and movement. This video contains information I've spent years acquiring and working into the realities and nuances of my life. I pray it makes the path toward healing a bit more serene and protected to navigate for those who take the time to watch it.

You can access both of these on my YouTube channel by using the QR code below:

Direct Link:
https://www.youtube.com/@cherylhollinshead6022

Milton Keynes UK
Ingram Content Group UK Ltd.
UKHW030656120324
439302UK00015B/897